Lunch Box Food

Sharon Dalgleish

Smart Apple Media

This edition first published in 2006 in the United States of America by Smart Apple Media.

Smart Apple Media
2140 Howard Drive West
North Mankato
Minnesota 56003

First published in 2006 by
MACMILLAN EDUCATION AUSTRALIA PTY LTD
627 Chapel Street, South Yarra, Australia 3141

Visit our Web site at www.macmillan.com.au

Associated companies and representatives throughout the world.

Library of Congress Cataloging-in-Publication Data

Dalgleish, Sharon.
   Lunch box food / by Sharon Dalgleish.
   p. cm. -- (Healthy choices)
   Includes index.
   ISBN-13: 978-1-58340-749-3
   1. Nutrition—Juvenile literature. 2. Lunchbox cookery—Juvenile literature. I. Title.

RA784.D34 2006
641.5'34—dc22

                                        2005057577

Edited by Helen Bethune Moore
Text and cover design by Christine Deering
Page layout by Domenic Lauricella
Photo research by Legend Images
Illustrations by Paul Konye

Printed in USA

Acknowledgments
The author and the publisher are grateful to the following for permission to reproduce copyright material:

Front cover: Boy and girl sharing lunch, courtesy of Image 100.

Brand X Pictures, pp. 10 (bottom right & bottom centre), 11 (top & bottom); Corbis Digital Stock, pp. 9 (top), 10 (bottom left), 11 (centre), 12 (bottom right), 23; Rob Cruse, pp. 13, 15 (left), 28; Digital Vision, pp. 9 (bottom), 11 (bottom left), 15 (right); Image100, p. 6; iStockphoto.com, pp. 4 (left), 27; MEA Photo, pp. 19 (right), 23 (left & right); Photodisc, pp. 1, 3, 7, 10 (top), 12 (top left & top centre), 14, 19 (left); Photolibrary RF, pp. 12 (top right & bottom left); Photolibrary/Plainpicture Gmbh & Co. Kg, pp. 4 (centre), 30; Photolibrary/Reso E.E.I.G, p. 4 (right); Photolibrary/Superstock, Inc., p. 18; Photolibrary/Veer, p. 26.

Contents

Healthy, fit, and happy

To be healthy, fit, and happy your body needs:

- a good mix of foods

- plenty of clean drinking water

- a **balance** of activity and rest

water

activity

A good mix of
foods, water, rest,
and play all help to
make you healthy.

mix of foods

Lunch box food

The food group pyramid can help you make healthy choices for your lunch box.

grains   vegetables   fruits   oils   dairy foods   meat and beans

The food group pyramid shows you which foods to eat most for a healthy, balanced diet.

Why make healthy choices?

Making healthy lunch box choices is important. A healthy lunch will give you **energy**. Your body needs energy to get through a busy school day.

A healthy lunch gives you energy to keep going all day.

You need to think hard at school so you can learn.
A healthy lunch will help you to think clearly.

A healthy lunch
helps you pay
attention in class.

Salads

Fruit and vegetables are full of **fiber** and **vitamins**. Fiber helps you **digest** food. Vitamins are **nutrients** and help keep diseases away.

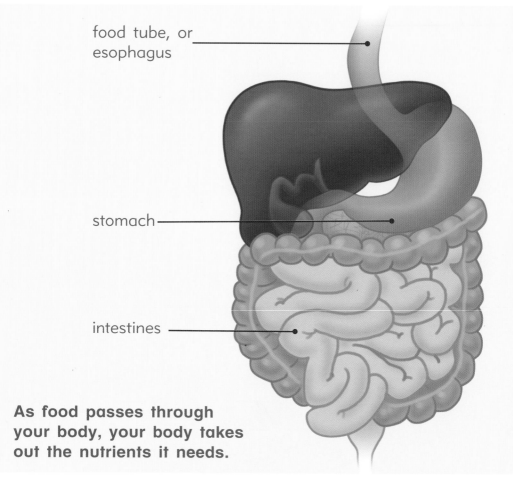

food tube, or
esophagus

stomach

intestines

As food passes through your body, your body takes out the nutrients it needs.

To be healthy, you need two pieces of fruit and four servings of vegetables each day. Packing fruit or vegetables in your lunch box helps you reach this target.

Three thin carrots are one serving of vegetables.

A banana is one serving of fruit.

Make a fruit salad

Ask a parent or teacher for help.

Take a home-made fruit salad to school. It is a good way to make sure you have enough fruit in your lunch.

Serves 1

What you need
- strawberries, grapes, pineapple, kiwi, mandarins, or your other favorite fruits
- a knife
- a peeler
- a small container with a lid

What to do
1 **Wash and dry the strawberries.**
2 **If you are using canned fruit, drain it.**
3 **Peel the other fruits, and chop large fruit into small pieces.**
4 **Place the fruit into the container and mix together.**

Make a vegetable salad

Ask a parent or teacher for help.

A fresh, crunchy salad is full of vitamins.

Serves 1

What you need

- carrot, lettuce, cherry tomatoes, snow peas, alfalfa sprouts, peppers, olives, or your other favorite vegetables, washed and dried
- a peeler
- a grater
- a small container with a lid

What to do

1 **Peel and grate the carrot.**

2 **Tear the lettuce into small pieces.**

3 **Mix the lettuce and the other vegetables together.**

4 **Place into the small container and mix together.**

Sandwiches, rolls, and wraps

Sandwiches, rolls, and wraps are different ways of using bread. Bread can be made from one type of **grain**, or from a mixture of grains. Grain gives you energy.

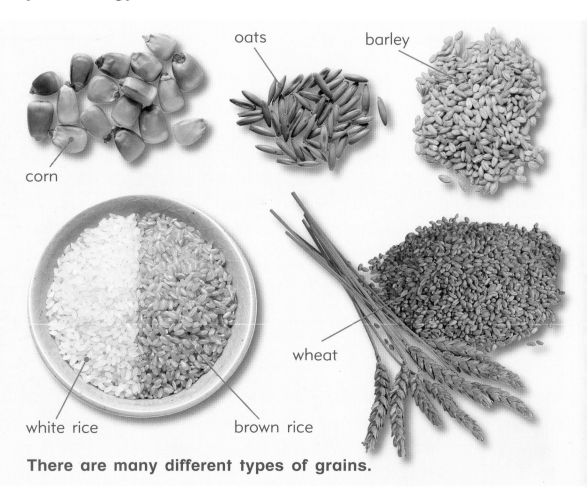

oats

barley

corn

white rice

brown rice

wheat

There are many different types of grains.

There are many different types of bread to choose from. Whole grain breads are best because they have more fiber to fill you up. Some white bread is good too.

Choose a different kind of bread to make your lunch more interesting.

Fillings

Choose a healthy filling for your sandwich. Meat, baked beans, or egg are a good choice. They contain **protein** and **iron**, and help your body build strong muscles.

A healthy protein filling in your sandwich is tasty and helps build your muscles.

Your sandwich does not have to be spread with butter. Try hummus, light mayonnaise, chutney, or ketchup instead. These spreads can give your body different nutrients.

tuna

egg

These fillings have protein. You only need two servings of protein a day.

Make a sandwich roll-up

Roll-ups can taste delicious. Try other fillings, such as grated cheese and raisins, or cottage cheese and alfalfa sprouts. Whatever you like!

What you need
- one slice of bread, crusts cut off
- light mayonnaise, small amount
- tuna, drained
- canned corn, drained
- a small bowl

What to do

1 Put the tuna, corn, and light mayonnaise into the bowl. Mix gently with the fork.

2 Spread the bread with the tuna mixture.

Ask a parent
or teacher
for help.

3 **Roll up the bread. Press together gently to keep it rolled up.**

4 **Cut the roll into three rounds.**

Treats

Your body needs only small amounts of sweet or fatty foods. Sweet foods can give you quick energy. Fatty foods can help make you feel full. Neither has many nutrients.

Advertisements on television can make you want to choose sweet or fatty foods.

Chips and candy are not the best treats to have in your lunch box. Other sweet-tasting choices can have less fat or sugar, and more nutrients.

muffins

homemade popcorn

These treats are healthier choices than chips and candy.

Make perfect pancakes

These pancakes make a perfect treat. Eat them plain, or spread them with honey.

Serves 4

What you need

- ½ cup wheat flour and ½ cup plain flour
- 1 cup milk
- 2 eggs
- oil or butter for cooking

- 2 bowls
- a jug
- a frying pan
- a teaspoon
- a wooden spoon
- a spatula

What to do

I **Mix the eggs and milk together in one bowl. Mix the flour in the other bowl and add the eggs and milk.**

2 **Use the wooden spoon to mix into a smooth batter. Pour the batter into a jug.**

Ask a parent or teacher for help.

3 Heat a frying pan and melt a teaspoon of oil or butter in it.

4 Pour in a little batter to make pancakes the size you want. Cook for about 2 minutes on each side, turning with the spatula.

Milky treats

Foods from the milk group give you calcium and other nutrients. Calcium helps to keep your bones and teeth strong and healthy.

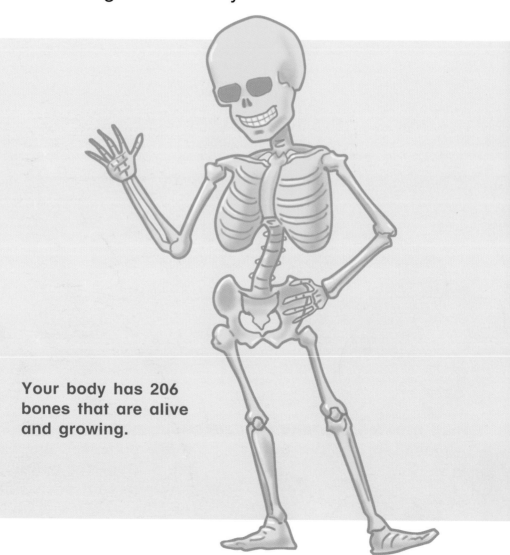

Your body has 206 bones that are alive and growing.

Milk group foods include cheese and yogurt, as well as milk. To be healthy, you need two to three servings from this group each day.

Cheese or yogurt makes a healthy milky treat.

Make a yogurt surprise

By lunch time, this yogurt surprise will be **thawed** but still nice and cold. Remember to pack a spoon.

What you need
- plain yogurt
- strawberries, blueberries, or mango
- small plastic container with a lid

What to do

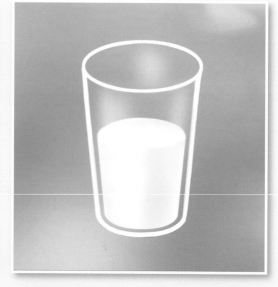

1 **Wash and dry the fruit. Cut large fruit into small pieces.**

2 **Half fill the small container with yogurt.**

Ask a parent or teacher for help.

3 **Add the fruit pieces and mix gently.**

4 **Put the lid onto the container and keep in the freezer overnight.**

Drinks

Do not forget to pack a drink in your lunch box. Water is the healthiest choice. It will stop you from getting **dehydrated**, especially on a hot day.

How much water do you need?	
Age	**You need**
5- to 8-year-olds	4 to 5 glasses of water a day
9- to 12-year-olds	6 to 7 glasses of water a day

Frozen water will melt by lunch time but still be nice and cold.

Fruit juice can make a nice change from fruit.
Be careful to choose a juice that has no added
sugar. Sugary drinks can make you thirstier.

**Freshly squeezed
orange juice is
delicious and has
no extra sugar.**

Keeping it fresh

A small, frozen icepack in your lunch box will keep the food cold and fresh. Milk, yogurt, cheese, eggs, and meat are best kept cool to be safe to eat.

Freezing your drink and packing it in your lunch box will keep your lunch cool.

Lunch box coolers

Keeping something cool in your lunch box will keep your food safe to eat. Try these frozen ideas.

Lunch box cooler ideas
Freeze a small carton of milk.
Freeze a tub of yogurt.
Cut an orange into quarters. Wrap in plastic cling wrap and freeze overnight.
Make a sandwich using frozen bread.
Wrap a fresh or tinned pineapple ring in plastic cling wrap and freeze.

Healthy choices for life

Making healthy choices in everything you do will help you to be fit, happy, and healthy.

Life is fun when you make healthy choices.

Glossary

balance   an equal amount of different things

calcium   a mineral found in food that helps build strong bones

dehydrated made sick because of lack of water

digest   to break down food and fluids inside the body

energy   strength to do things

fiber   found in plant foods, and helps your body break down food

grain   the hard seeds of cereals

iron   a mineral found in food that helps carry oxygen around your body

nutrients   healthy substances found in food, such as vitamins and minerals

protein   a substance found in food that builds muscles

thawed   melted; to stop being frozen

vitamins   healthy substances found in food

Index